Medieval Rulers

by Grace Hansen

Abdo
THE MIDDLE AGES
Kids

Abdo Kids Jumbo is an Imprint of Abdo Kids
abdobooks.com

abdobooks.com

Published by Abdo Kids, a division of ABDO, P.O. Box 398166, Minneapolis, Minnesota 55439.

Printed in the United States of America, North Mankato, Minnesota.

052025

092025

THIS BOOK CONTAINS RECYCLED MATERIALS

Photo Credits: Alamy, Getty Images, Granger Collection, Shutterstock

Production Contributors: Teddy Borth, Jennie Forsberg, Grace Hansen
Design Contributors: Candice Keimig, Pakou Moua

Library of Congress Control Number: 2024947615

Publisher's Cataloging-in-Publication Data

Names: Hansen, Grace, author.

Title: Medieval rulers / by Grace Hansen

Description: Minneapolis, Minnesota : Abdo Kids, 2026 | Series: The Middle Ages | Includes online resources and index.

Identifiers: ISBN 9798384905332 (lib. bdg.) | ISBN 9798384906032 (ebook) | ISBN 9798384906384 (Read-to-me ebook)

Subjects: LCSH: Kings and rulers--Juvenile literature. | Dynasties (Royal houses)--Juvenile literature. | Middle Ages--Juvenile literature. | Medieval history--Juvenile literature. | Dark Ages--Juvenile literature.

Classification: DDC 940.1--dc23

Table of Contents

The Middle Ages

The Middle Ages, or medieval period, was a time in European history. It lasted from about 500 to 1500 CE. Many important rulers lived during this time.

Europe
Asia
Africa

Medieval Kings & Queens

King Charlemagne was King of the **Franks** from 768 until his death in 814. Charlemagne united much of Europe under his rule.

King
Charlemagne
England
The
Netherlands
Germany
Belgium
Luxembourg
Charlemagne's
Empire
Austria
France
Switzerland
Europe
Slovenia
Italy
Spain
N
W
E
S

William the Conqueror ruled Normandy and England until 1087. He **invaded** England in 1066 and was crowned king. He built hundreds of castles during his **reign**.

William
the Conqueror
England
Castles built by William
Warwick Castle
England

Eleanor of Aquitaine was the Queen of France and England in her lifetime. She married King Henry II in 1152. They had 8 children. She supported her sons in **dethroning** their father. She went to prison until the death of Henry II.

Eleanor
of Aquitaine
King
Henry II
The children of Eleanor and Henry II
J.C. Buttre

Richard I was the son of Eleanor and Henry II. He ruled from 1189 to 1199. He was a great warrior and military leader. Because of this, he was known as Richard the Lionheart.

Richard
the Lionheart

Robert I, or Robert the Bruce, was the King of Scots from 1306 to 1329. He led the Scottish fight for **independence**. Scotland won its independence from England in 1328.

Robert
the Bruce
Scotland
England

Henry V was one of England's most popular kings. He ruled from 1413 to 1422. He led the country to many victories in the **Hundred Years' War** against France.

Henry V

Margaret of Anjou married Henry VI of England in 1445. The King was often unwell, so Margaret ruled in his place. She even led the king's army in battle during the **Wars of the Roses**.

Henry VI
Margaret
of Anjou

Isabella I of Castile was one of the most powerful women of the Middle Ages. In her 20-year rule, she helped unite Spain.

England
Europe
France
Portugal
Spain
Isabella I
of Castile
Christopher
Columbus

Where in Europe?

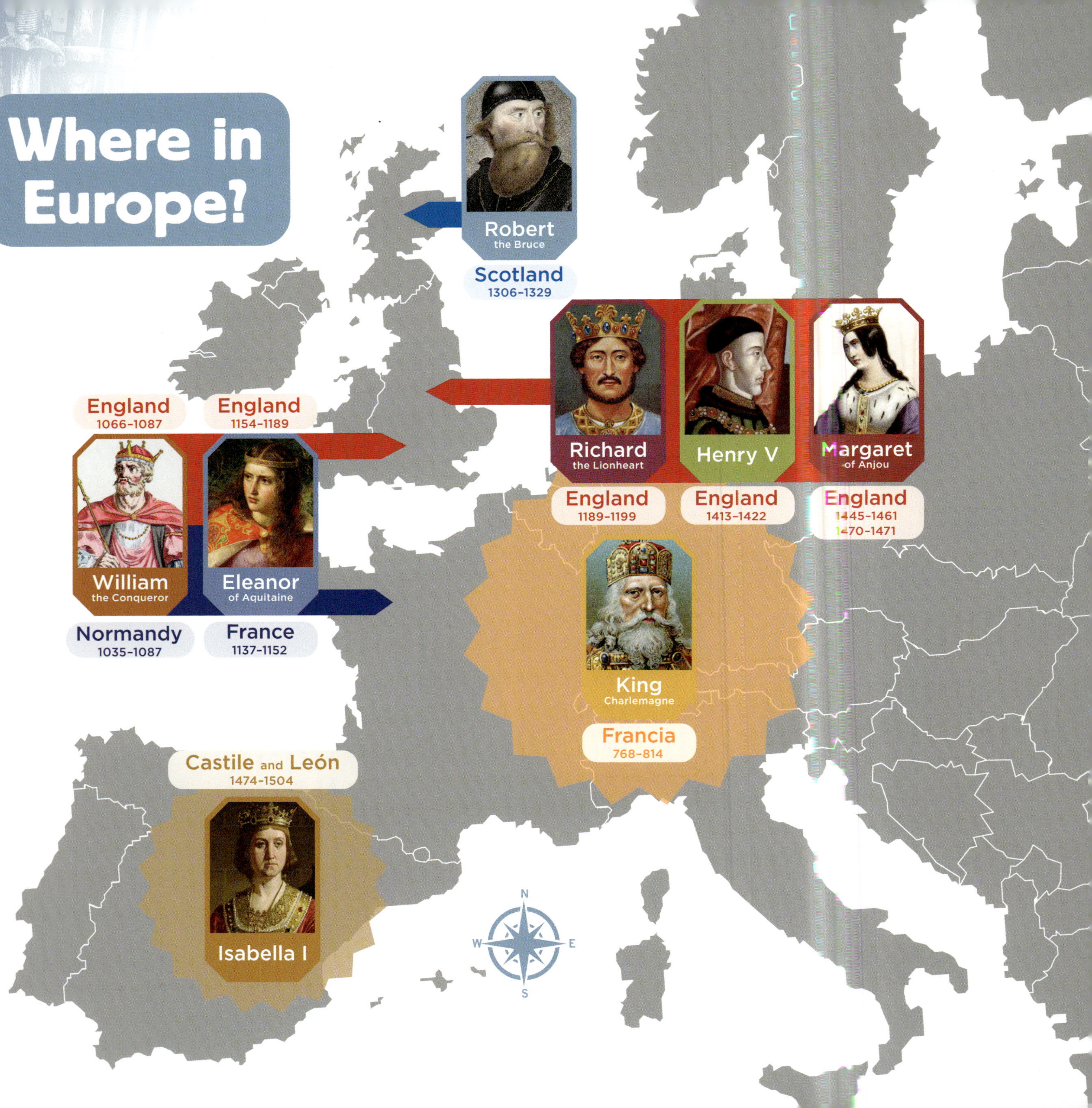

Glossary

dethrone – to remove from the throne or other high and powerful position.

Franks – a group of people who lived in western Europe in the early Middle Ages.

Hundred Years' War – a longtime conflict, lasting from 1337 to 1453, between the kingdoms of England and France. In the end, France claimed victory.

independence – freedom from outside control.

invade – to enter as an enemy and take over by force.

reign – rule of a king or queen.

Wars of the Roses – a series of civil wars, lasting from about 1455 to 1485, fought in England between the House of York (represented by the white rose) and the House of Lancaster (represented by the red rose) for control of the English throne.

Index